# THE INDIAN MYTHOLOGY

## A MODERN INTERPRETATION OF THE ANCIENT HINDU MYTHS

## DR. JAGADEESH PILLAI

|| Dedicated to all wisdom seekers around the world ||

# Contents

# Contents

# Prayer



The literal meaning of this mantra is: OM. O Gods! Let us hear auspicious words from our ears. O reverent Gods! Let us behold propitious visions from our eyes, let our organs and body be stable, healthy, and strong. Let us do that which is pleasing to the gods in the life span allotted to us. May Indra, inscribed in the scriptures, bring us fortune! May Pushan, the knower of the world, grant us prosperity! May Trakshya, who vanquishes enemies, bestow us with blessings! May Brihaspati bring us success!
OM Peace, Peace, Peace.

# About The Author

Dr. Jagadeesh Pillai is a renowned Guinness World Record holder, writer, and researcher hailing from Varanasi, also known as the abode of Lord Shiva. With a Ph.D. in Vedic Science and a range of creative ideas and achievements, he is a true polymath. He is the author of more than 100 books including Research Publications. Although his roots can be traced back to Kerala, the people of Varanasi hold him in high regard and affectionately consider him one of their own.

Dr. Pillai has achieved four Guinness World Records in the following subjects:

**"Script to Screen"** - In this record, Dr. Pillai produced and directed an animation film within the shortest time possible, breaking the previous record set by Canadians. He has also received numerous national and international awards and recognitions for this achievement.

**Longest Line of Postcards** - For this record, Dr. Pillai created a line of 16,300 postcards on the occasion of the $163^{rd}$ anniversary of Indian Postal Day. The event also included a questionnaire about the Indian flag.

**Largest Poster Awareness Campaign** - Dr. Pillai designed an awareness campaign on the subject of "Beti Bachao - Beti Padhao" (Save the Girl Child - Educate the Girl Child) to achieve this record.

**Largest Envelope** - In tribute to the Indian Prime Minister's

"Make in India" initiative, Dr. Pillai created a 4000 square meter envelope using waste paper to achieve this record.

Attempted - **70000 Candles on a 210 kg Cake** - To celebrate the 70th Indian Independence Day, Dr. Pillai attempted to light 70,000 candles on a 210 kg cake, which was recorded in World Records India.

Attempted - **Documentary on Dhamek Stupa of Sarnath in 17 Languages** - Dr. Pillai attempted to create a documentary on the Dhamek Stupa of Sarnath, dubbing it in 17 different languages. The result of this attempt is currently awaiting confirmation from the Guinness World Records.

Dr. Pillai is skilled in teaching the Bhagavad Gita, a Hindu scripture, and is popular among young people. He has helped many young people improve their lives through his motivational teachings.

In addition to teaching, he has composed and sung numerous Sanskrit Bhajans and patriotic songs.

He has also written and directed several short films and documentaries for awareness campaigns, and has volunteered with the police in both UP and Kerala to spread awareness about various issues through videos and photography.

Incredibly, he has produced and directed over 100 documentaries about the city of Varanasi, all on his own.

He has also helped and guided more than 25 boys and girls to achieve world records through creative and innovative methods. He is a multifaceted person who uses his intellect and the blessings given to him by God to excel in various areas. He is both a teacher and a student, always learning and teaching, and is able to master any subject he comes across.

He is a selfless social activist and motivational speaker who has overcome struggles and failures to become a successful and enthusiastic individual with a rich life experience.

In addition to his work with the Bhagavad Gita, he is also an efficient Tarot card reader, Astro-Vastu consultant, and a talented singer and composer. He has sung the entire Ram Charita Manas and Bhagavad Gita in his own compositions, and has sung the phrase "Lokah Samastha Sukhino Bhavantu" in 50 different languages. He is currently working on a detailed and scientific study of Vedas, Upanishads, Puranas, and the Bhagavad Gita. He has also composed and sung the Hanuman Chalisa and Gayatri Mantra in 108 and 1008 different compositions, respectively.

Awards - Four Times Guinness World Records, Winner of Mahatma Gandhi Vishwa Shanti Puraskar, Mahatma Gandhi Global Peace Ambassador, Kashi Ratna Award, Dr. APJ Abdul Kalam Motivational Person of the Year 2017, Mother Teresa Award, Indira Gandhi Priyadarshini Award, Bharat Vikas Ratna Award, Udyog Ratna Award, Vigyan Prasar Award, Poorvanchal Ratn Samman.

# PREFACE

The Indian Mythology: A Modern Interpretation of The Ancient Hindu Myths is a book that delves into the rich and complex tradition of Indian mythology. This book explores the stories and characters from Indian mythology, their origins, and their ongoing relevance and significance in modern times.

The book begins with an introduction to Indian mythology, providing an overview of the different types of myths and their origins. It then delves into the Vedic myths, which include creation stories and cosmology, and the epics, the Ramayana and the Mahabharata. The book also explores the Puranas and the tales of the deities, including the Trimurti and the Devi, as well as the Avatars of Vishnu.

One of the key themes of the book is the reinterpretation and modern interpretation of Indian myths. The book explores various modern interpretations such as psychological, feminist, ecological and postcolonial perspectives, which offer new insights into these ancient stories and their relevance in the modern world.

The book also examines the influence of Indian mythology in art and literature, highlighting how these ancient stories have been depicted in various forms of art and have been a major source of inspiration for poets, playwrights, and novelists. The book also explores the incorporation of Indian mythology into popular culture, such as movies, television shows, comics, and video games.

The book concludes with a discussion of the comparisons and connections between Indian mythology and other mythological traditions around the world, highlighting the universal human experiences reflected in Indian myths and the role of myths in shaping cultural beliefs and practices.

This book is intended for readers who are interested in Indian culture, mythology, and spirituality, as well as for those who want to gain a deeper understanding of the human experience and the role that myths play in shaping cultural beliefs and practices. It is a comprehensive guide to Indian mythology, providing a modern interpretation of these ancient stories and highlighting their ongoing relevance and significance in today's world.

# I

# The Indian Mythology: A Modern Interpretation of The Ancient Hindu Myths

Indian mythology is a rich tapestry of stories, beliefs, and traditions that have been passed down through generations. It is an integral part of the Indian culture and has played a significant role in shaping the country's history, society, and worldview. The myths and legends of India are deeply rooted in the country's spiritual and religious traditions, and they offer a window into the ancient Indian mind and its understanding of the world around it.

The Indian mythology is primarily based on the religious texts of Hinduism, which are known as the Vedas. These texts, which were written over 2,000 years ago, contain a vast collection of myths, legends, and stories that describe the origins of the universe, the nature of the gods, and the moral and ethical principles that govern human life. The Vedas are considered to be the sacred texts of Hinduism and are still studied and revered by scholars and practitioners of the religion today.

One of the most important figures in Indian mythology is Lord Vishnu, who is considered to be the preserver and protector of the universe. According to Hindu belief, Lord Vishnu is one of the three main gods of the Hindu pantheon, along with Lord Brahma and Lord Shiva. Lord Vishnu is often depicted as a blue-skinned, four-armed deity holding a conch shell, a discus, a mace, and a lotus flower. He is often accompanied by his consort, the goddess Lakshmi, who is the goddess of wealth and prosperity.

Another important figure in Indian mythology is Lord Shiva, who is considered to be the destroyer and transformer of the universe. Lord Shiva is often depicted as a fierce, blue-skinned deity with a third eye on his forehead and a snake around his neck. He is often accompanied by his consort, the goddess Parvati, who is the goddess of power and fertility.

In addition to Lord Vishnu and Lord Shiva, there are many other gods and goddesses in Indian mythology, each with their own unique attributes and powers. For example, there is Lord Ganesha, the elephant-headed god of wisdom and success, and Lord Hanuman, the monkey god of strength and devotion.

The Indian mythology also contains a wide variety of stories and legends that are meant to teach moral and ethical lessons. For example, the story of Lord Rama, who is considered to be an incarnation of Lord Vishnu, teaches the importance of duty, loyalty, and self-sacrifice. The story of Lord Krishna, who is also considered to be an incarnation of Lord Vishnu, teaches the importance of love, compassion, and devotion.

Indian mythology is a vast and complex field that encompasses a wide range of stories, beliefs, and traditions. It is deeply rooted in the spiritual and religious traditions of India and offers a unique window into the ancient Indian mind and its understanding of the world around it. It is a rich tapestry that continues to inspire and inform the lives of millions of people around the world.

*"Indian mythology is the mirror in which the mind of ancient India looked at itself."*

\- Romila Thapar

# II

# The Vedic Myths: Creation and Cosmology

The Vedic myths are a collection of stories, beliefs, and traditions that are found in the ancient Hindu texts known as the Vedas. These texts, which were written over 2,000 years ago, contain a vast collection of myths, legends, and stories that describe the origins of the universe, the nature of the gods, and the moral and ethical principles that govern human life.

One of the most important themes in the Vedic myths is the creation of the universe. According to these myths, the universe was created by the god Brahma, who is considered to be the creator of the world. Brahma is often depicted as a four-headed deity who emerged from a cosmic egg, also known as the Golden Egg. From this egg, Brahma created the elements that make up the universe, including the sky, the earth, and the oceans.

Another important theme in the Vedic myths is the concept of cosmology. The Vedas describe a cyclical process of creation and destruction, known as the cycle of the yugas. According to this belief, the universe goes through a series of cycles, with each cycle lasting for thousands of years. Each cycle is divided into four yugas, or ages, known as the Satya Yuga, the Treta Yuga, the Dvapara Yuga, and the Kali Yuga. The Satya Yuga is considered to be the golden age, where people live in peace and harmony. As the cycle progresses, the yugas become increasingly darker, with the Kali Yuga being the age of chaos and destruction.

The Vedic myths also describe a complex pantheon of gods and goddesses, each with their own unique attributes and powers. For example, the god Indra is considered to be the king of the gods and the god of thunder and rain. The god Agni is considered to be the god of fire and is often invoked in rituals and ceremonies. The goddess Saraswati is considered to be the goddess of wisdom and learning.

The Vedic myths are a rich and complex collection of stories, beliefs, and traditions that are deeply rooted in the spiritual and religious traditions of ancient India. They describe the origins of the universe, the nature of the gods, and the moral and ethical principles that govern human life. They provide a unique window into the ancient Indian mind and its understanding of the world around it.

"The stories of Indian mythology are not just ancient tales, but a reflection of the human experience."

# III

# The Epics: The Ramayana and the Mahabharata

The Ramayana and the Mahabharata are two of the most famous epics in Indian mythology. Both epics are considered to be the cornerstones of Indian literature and have been passed down through generations in the form of stories, plays, and performances. They contain a wealth of information about the beliefs, customs, and traditions of ancient India.

The Ramayana is an epic poem that tells the story of Prince Rama and his quest to rescue his wife Sita from the demon king, Ravana. The story is divided into seven books and narrates the life of Rama, from his birth and childhood to his exile and eventual return to his kingdom. Along the way, Rama faces many challenges and obstacles, but with the help of his loyal brother, Lakshmana, and the monkey god,

Hanuman, he is ultimately able to rescue Sita and defeat Ravana. The Ramayana is considered to be one of the greatest works of Indian literature and is still widely read and performed today.

The Mahabharata is another epic poem that tells the story of the Kuru dynasty, a powerful family in ancient India. The story is divided into 18 books and tells the story of the Kuru prince, Bhisma, and his descendants. The epic is centered around a great war between the Kuru family and their cousins, the Pandavas, which ultimately leads to the death of nearly all the main characters. The Mahabharata is considered to be one of the longest epic poems in the world and is considered to be one of the greatest works of Indian literature. It is also a source of teachings on dharma, artha, kama, and moksha.

Both the Ramayana and the Mahabharata are considered to be important texts in the Hindu religion and are still widely read and studied today. They contain a wealth of information about the beliefs, customs, and traditions of ancient India and offer a unique window into the ancient Indian mind and its understanding of the world around it. Additionally, they are great examples of ancient Indian epic poetry and are considered to be some of the most important works of literature in the world.

*"The characters and events in Indian mythology represent aspects of the human psyche, providing insights into human behavior."*

॰

# IV

# The Puranas and the Tales of the Deities

The Puranas are a collection of ancient texts in Hinduism that contain a wide variety of stories, myths, and legends. These texts are believed to have been written between 300 BCE and 300 CE and are considered to be an important source of information about the beliefs, customs, and traditions of ancient India. The Puranas are divided into 18 major texts, each of which is dedicated to a specific deity or group of deities.

The Puranas contain a wide variety of stories about the gods and goddesses of the Hindu pantheon. For example, the Vishnu Purana tells the story of Lord Vishnu and his various incarnations, including his life as Lord Rama and Lord Krishna. The Shiva Purana tells the story of Lord Shiva and his consort, the goddess Parvati. The Devi Mahatmya, which is part of the Markandeya Purana, is a powerful text that describes the goddess as the ultimate reality and power behind all of creation.

In addition to the stories of the gods and goddesses, the Puranas also contain a wealth of information about the beliefs, customs, and traditions of ancient India. For example, the Puranas describe the importance of the caste system, the duties of the different classes of society, and the importance of performing religious rituals and ceremonies. They also contain information about the different hells and heavens, and the different types of souls and their ultimate fate.

The tales of the deities in the Puranas are often used to convey moral and ethical lessons, and to teach people about the nature of the universe and the meaning of life. They also provide a window into the ancient Indian mind and its understanding of the world around it. The stories of the gods and goddesses, as well as the information about the beliefs, customs, and traditions of ancient India, make the Puranas an important source of knowledge about the history, culture, and religion of India.

The Puranas are a collection of ancient texts in Hinduism that contain a wide variety of stories, myths, and legends about the gods and goddesses of the Hindu pantheon, as well as information about the beliefs, customs, and traditions of ancient India. They are considered to be an important source of knowledge about the history, culture, and religion of India and are still widely read and studied today.

DR. JAGADEESH PILLAI

*"The gods and goddesses in Indian mythology are not just deities, but symbols of universal human emotions and experiences."*

# V

# The Trimurti: Brahma, Vishnu and Shiva

The Trimurti is a concept in Hinduism that refers to the three main deities of the Hindu pantheon: Brahma, Vishnu, and Shiva. These three gods are considered to be the creators, preservers, and destroyers of the universe, respectively. They are often depicted as a triad, with Brahma as the creator, Vishnu as the preserver, and Shiva as the destroyer.

Brahma, also known as the Creator God, is considered to be the creator of the universe. According to Hindu belief, Brahma emerged from the cosmic egg and created the elements that make up the universe, including the sky, the earth, and the oceans. He is often depicted as having four heads, symbolizing the four cardinal directions. He is also associated with the sacred Hindu syllable OM, which is considered to be the sound of creation.

Vishnu, also known as the Preserver God, is considered to be the preserver of the universe. According to Hindu belief, Vishnu maintains the balance of the universe and ensures that the world continues to exist. He is often depicted as a blue-skinned deity with four arms, holding a conch shell, a discus, a mace, and a lotus flower. He is often accompanied by his consort, the goddess Lakshmi, who is the goddess of wealth and prosperity. Vishnu has also taken several incarnations or avatars to preserve the balance of the world, for example, Rama and Krishna.

Shiva, also known as the Destroyer God, is considered to be the destroyer of the universe. According to Hindu belief, Shiva destroys the world in order to make way for a new creation. He is often depicted as a fierce, blue-skinned deity with a third eye on his forehead and a snake around his neck. He is often accompanied by his consort, the goddess Parvati, who is the goddess of power and fertility. Shiva is also associated with the practice of yoga and is considered to be the patron of ascetics and yogis.

The Trimurti is a concept in Hinduism that refers to the three main deities of the Hindu pantheon: Brahma, Vishnu, and Shiva. These three gods are considered to be the creators, preservers, and destroyers of the universe, respectively. They are often depicted as a triad, with Brahma as the creator, Vishnu as the preserver, and Shiva as the destroyer. Each god has a specific role and function in the maintenance of the universe, and they are all revered and worshiped by Hindus across the world.

*"Indian mythology is not just a collection of stories, but a rich source of wisdom and guidance for living a virtuous life."*

# VI

# The Devi: The Goddess in Indian Mythology

The Devi, also known as the goddess, is a central figure in Indian mythology. She is considered to be the ultimate reality and power behind all of creation. The Devi is revered and worshiped in many forms, and has many different names and manifestations.

One of the most popular forms of the Devi is as the goddess Durga. She is considered to be the mother of the universe and is often depicted as a powerful warrior goddess, riding a lion or a tiger and carrying weapons in her many arms. Durga is known as the goddess who protects her devotees from evil and negative forces, and is often invoked during times of war and conflict.

Another popular form of the Devi is as the goddess

Lakshmi. She is considered to be the goddess of wealth and prosperity and is often depicted as a beautiful woman, surrounded by gold coins and jewels. Lakshmi is associated with good luck and is often invoked by people seeking financial success or material wealth.

The Devi is also worshiped as the goddess Kali. She is considered to be the goddess of destruction and is often depicted as a fierce, dark-skinned woman, with wild hair and a necklace of skulls. Kali is associated with death and rebirth, and is often invoked during rituals related to death and the afterlife.

The Devi is also revered as the goddess of knowledge and learning, as the goddess of power, as the goddess of fertility and many other aspects of life. The Devi is not just confined to one particular form, and she can manifest in any form that is needed.

The Devi is a central figure in Indian mythology and is considered to be the ultimate reality and power behind all of creation. She is revered and worshiped in many forms and has many different names and manifestations. She is known as the mother of the universe and is often depicted as a powerful warrior goddess, a goddess of wealth and prosperity, a goddess of death and rebirth and many other aspects of life. The Devi is not just confined to one particular form, and she can manifest in any form that is needed, making her the ultimate and all-encompassing goddess of the Hindu pantheon.

"The study of Indian mythology allows us to understand the evolution of human beliefs and values."

൬

# VII

# The Avatars of Vishnu: Rama, Krishna, and more

The avatars of Vishnu are the incarnations or manifestations of the Hindu god Vishnu in human or animal form. According to Hindu belief, Vishnu takes on an avatar in order to restore balance to the world and to protect the righteous from evil. The most famous avatars of Vishnu are Rama and Krishna, but there are many other avatars as well.

Rama is considered to be the seventh avatar of Vishnu and is the central character in the Hindu epic Ramayana. According to the story, Rama is the prince of Ayodhya who is exiled to the forest for 14 years. He is accompanied by his wife, Sita, and his brother, Lakshmana. During his exile, Rama faces many challenges and obstacles, but with the help of his loyal followers, he is ultimately able to rescue

Sita and defeat the demon king, Ravana. Rama is considered to be an ideal human being, and his story is often used to teach moral and ethical lessons.

Krishna is considered to be the eighth avatar of Vishnu and is the central character in the Hindu epic Mahabharata. According to the story, Krishna is a prince who becomes the advisor and friend of the Pandavas, the five sons of Pandu. He helps them in their battle against their cousins, the Kauravas, and ultimately helps them to win the war. Krishna is considered to be a divine figure, and his story is often used to teach people about the nature of the universe and the meaning of life.

Other avatars of Vishnu include Matsya, the fish, Kurma, the turtle, Varaha, the boar, Narasimha, the man-lion, Vamana, the dwarf, Parasurama, the warrior with an axe and Kalki, the final avatar who is yet to come. Each avatar has their own unique story and purpose, and they are all revered and worshiped by Hindus across the world.

The avatars of Vishnu are the incarnations or manifestations of the Hindu god Vishnu in human or animal form. The most famous avatars of Vishnu are Rama and Krishna, but there are many other avatars as well. Each avatar has their own unique story and purpose, and they are all revered and worshiped by Hindus across the world. They are considered to be powerful and benevolent figures who come to the world to restore balance and protect the righteous from evil. The avatars of Vishnu are an important part of Hindu mythology and continue to inspire and inform the lives of millions of people around the world.

ಜ

"The reinterpretation of Indian myths through a feminist lens offers a new perspective on the portrayal of women in ancient stories."

# VIII

# The Ramayana: The Story of Rama

The Ramayana is an ancient Indian epic poem that tells the story of Prince Rama and his quest to rescue his wife Sita from the demon king, Ravana. The story is divided into seven books and narrates the life of Rama, from his birth and childhood to his exile and eventual return to his kingdom.

The story begins with the birth of Rama, the prince of Ayodhya, and his childhood. Rama is the eldest son of King Dasharatha and is considered to be the ideal human being. He is known for his bravery, strength, and wisdom. He is also known for his devotion to his family and his duty as a prince.

When Rama grows up, his father decides to crown him as the king of Ayodhya. But his stepmother, Kaikeyi, who wants her own son Bharata to be king, convinces King

Dasharatha to send Rama into exile for 14 years. Rama, along with his wife Sita and his brother Lakshmana, goes into exile in the forest.

In the forest, Rama faces many challenges and obstacles. He fights against demons and monsters and also encounters many sages and ascetics. During their exile, Sita is kidnapped by the demon king Ravana, who wants to marry her. Rama and Lakshmana, with the help of Hanuman, a monkey god and a loyal follower of Rama, set out to rescue Sita. They gather an army of monkeys and bears and march towards Lanka, the kingdom of Ravana.

The final battle between Rama and Ravana is intense and brutal, but in the end, Rama emerges victorious and rescues Sita. However, upon returning to Ayodhya, Sita's reputation is questioned due to her time spent in Ravana's captivity. To prove her innocence, Sita undergoes a test of fire and emerges unscathed, proving her purity. Rama and Sita are then crowned as king and queen of Ayodhya.

The story of Rama is not just a tale of adventure and war, but also of love, loyalty, and duty. Rama is considered to be an ideal human being, and his story is often used to teach moral and ethical lessons. The Ramayana is considered to be one of the greatest works of Indian literature and is still widely read and performed today. It is a source of inspiration for many and serves as a guide for living a virtuous life.

"Indian mythology reflects a deep
understanding and respect for the natural
world, providing important messages about
living in harmony with nature."

ෆ

# IX

# The Mahabharata: The Story of the Pandavas

The Mahabharata is an ancient Indian epic poem that tells the story of the Kuru dynasty, a powerful family in ancient India. The story is divided into 18 books and tells the story of the Kuru prince, Bhisma, and his descendants, particularly the five Pandava brothers - Yudhishthira, Bhima, Arjuna, Nakula and Sahadeva, and their struggle for the throne with their cousins, the Kauravas. The epic is set in the city of Hastinapura, where the Kuru family lives.

The story begins with the rivalry between the Pandavas and the Kauravas, who are the sons of Bhisma's brother, Dhritarashtra. The Kauravas, led by their eldest brother Duryodhana, are jealous of the Pandavas and their growing power and popularity. They hatch a plan to eliminate the Pandavas by inviting them to a game of dice, in which the

Pandavas end up losing everything, including their kingdom and freedom.

The Pandavas are forced into exile for 13 years, during which they face many challenges and obstacles. They also gain powerful allies, such as Lord Krishna, who becomes a mentor and advisor to the Pandavas. After 13 years, the Pandavas return to Hastinapura and claim their rightful place on the throne. However, the Kauravas refuse to give up the kingdom and a great war ensues between the two sides.

The war is fierce and brutal, and many lives are lost on both sides. The Pandavas ultimately emerge victorious, but at a great cost. Almost all the main characters, including Bhisma, Drona, and both the Pandavas and the Kauravas, are killed in the war. The Pandavas, the last surviving members of the Kuru dynasty, decide to renounce their kingdom and embark on a journey to the Himalayas to attain salvation.

The Mahabharata is considered to be one of the longest epic poems in the world and is considered to be one of the greatest works of Indian literature. It is also a source of teachings on dharma, artha, kama, and moksha, the four goals of human life in Hinduism. The story of the Pandavas is not just a tale of war and politics, but also of family, loyalty, and duty. The Mahabharata serves as a reminder of the consequences of greed, jealousy, and the importance of living a virtuous life. It continues to be widely read and studied today and is an integral part of the cultural heritage of India.

ॐ

"The influence of Indian mythology in art and literature is a testament to its enduring relevance and appeal."

# X
# Myths and Legends of the Deities

Indian mythology is rich with myths and legends about the deities. These stories are often used to convey moral and ethical lessons, and to teach people about the nature of the universe and the meaning of life. Some of the most popular myths and legends of the deities include:

**The story of the god Shiva and the goddess Parvati:** This is a popular myth that tells the story of how the god Shiva and the goddess Parvati fell in love and got married. According to the myth, Shiva was a fierce and powerful god who was known for his asceticism and detachment. He was not interested in love or marriage, but Parvati was determined to win his heart. She performed austerities and penances to please him and finally succeeded in winning his love. The myth is often used to teach people about the power of devotion and the importance of perseverance.

**The story of the god Vishnu and the goddess Lakshmi:** This is a myth that tells the story of how the god Vishnu and the goddess Lakshmi fell in love and got married. According to the myth, Vishnu was a kind and benevolent god who was known for his compassion and generosity. He was not interested in love or marriage, but Lakshmi was determined to win his heart. She performed austerities and penances to please him and finally succeeded in winning his love. The myth is often used to teach people about the power of devotion and the importance of perseverance.

**The story of the god Ganesha and the goddess Saraswati:** This is a myth that tells the story of how the god Ganesha and the goddess Saraswati fell in love and got married. According to the myth, Ganesha was a wise and learned god who was known for his intelligence and knowledge. He was not interested in love or marriage, but Saraswati was determined to win his heart. She performed austerities and penances to please him and finally succeeded in winning his love. The myth is often used to teach people about the power of devotion and the importance of perseverance.

Indian mythology is rich with myths and legends about the deities, these stories are often used to convey moral and ethical lessons, and to teach people about the nature of the universe and the meaning of life. These myths and legends are still widely read and studied today and continue to inspire and inform the lives of people around the world.

"The comparisons and connections between Indian mythology and other mythological traditions highlight the universal human experiences reflected in myths."

༄

# XI

# The Influence of Indian Mythology in art and literature

Indian mythology has had a significant influence on art and literature in India. The stories and characters from mythology have been depicted in various forms of art such as paintings, sculptures, and architecture. The intricate carvings and sculptures of Hindu gods and goddesses can be found in many temples and shrines across India, and are considered to be some of the finest examples of Indian art.

In literature, Indian mythology has been a major source of inspiration for poets, playwrights, and novelists. The stories and characters from mythology have been retold in various forms, including poetry, plays, and novels. The Ramayana and the Mahabharata, two of the most famous Indian epics, have been retold in various languages and have been adapted into plays and films.

In addition, Indian mythology has also had a significant influence on Indian music and dance. Many classical Indian dance forms, such as Bharatanatyam, Kathak, and Kathakali, are based on stories and characters from mythology. Similarly, Indian classical music is also heavily influenced by mythology, with many compositions based on the stories and characters from mythology.

In modern times, Indian mythology continues to be a popular source of inspiration for artists and writers. Many contemporary artists and writers have been influenced by Indian mythology, and have used stories and characters from mythology in their work. This has allowed Indian mythology to reach a wider audience and continue to be a major cultural influence in India and around the world.

Indian mythology has had a significant influence on art and literature in India. The stories and characters from mythology have been depicted in various forms of art such as paintings, sculptures, and architecture. In literature, Indian mythology has been a major source of inspiration for poets, playwrights, and novelists. Indian mythology has also had a significant influence on Indian music and dance. In modern times, Indian mythology continues to be a popular source of inspiration for artists and writers and it continues to be a major cultural influence in India and around the world.

*"The incorporation of Indian mythology into popular culture has helped to bring these ancient stories to a wider audience."*

৪৩

# XII

# Reinterpretations and Modern Interpretations of Indian Myths

Indian myths have been retold and interpreted in various ways throughout history. In recent times, there have been many reinterpretations and modern interpretations of Indian myths that have attempted to bring new perspectives and insights to these ancient stories.

One modern interpretation of Indian myths is the psychological interpretation, which tries to understand the deeper meanings and symbolism behind the stories. This interpretation suggests that the characters and events in the myths represent aspects of the human psyche, such as the ego, the shadow, and the anima/animus. This interpretation has been used to understand the inner workings of the human mind and to provide insights into human behavior.

Another modern interpretation of Indian myths is the feminist interpretation, which focuses on the roles and representation of women in the myths. This interpretation suggests that the myths reflect patriarchal values and attitudes towards women, and that they often portray women in a negative or subservient light. Feminist scholars have attempted to reinterpret these myths to provide a more positive and empowering portrayal of women.

A third modern interpretation is the ecological interpretation. This interpretation focuses on the relationship between humans and nature in Indian myths. This interpretation suggests that Indian myths reflect a deep understanding and respect for the natural world, and that they contain important messages about the importance of living in harmony with nature.

Lastly, a postcolonial interpretation of Indian myths has been developed. This interpretation focus on how myths were used to justify the colonization and oppression of native peoples. By examining how myths were used to justify these actions, scholars can better understand the impact of colonialism on native cultures and societies.

Indian myths have been retold and interpreted in various ways throughout history. In recent times, there have been many reinterpretations and modern interpretations of Indian myths that have attempted to bring new perspectives and insights to these ancient stories. Some of these interpretations include psychological, feminist, ecological and postcolonial. These interpretations have been used to better understand the human psyche, to empower women, to understand the relationship between humans and nature, and to understand the impact of colonialism on native cultures and societies.

"The stories of Indian mythology are not just
myths but they are the mirror of our society
and culture."


৪৩

# XIII

# Indian Mythology in Pop culture

Indian mythology has played a significant role in popular culture, both in India and internationally. Many aspects of Indian mythology have been adapted and incorporated into various forms of popular culture, such as movies, television shows, comics, and video games.

One of the most notable examples of Indian mythology in popular culture is the adaptation of the Ramayana and the Mahabharata into movies and television shows. These epic stories have been adapted into various languages and have been popular in India and around the world. Many Bollywood movies and TV series have been based on the stories of Ramayana and Mahabharata.

Another way Indian mythology has been incorporated into pop culture is through the use of mythological characters and themes in comics and graphic novels. Many popular comics and graphic novels feature characters and stories inspired by Indian mythology.

In recent years, Indian mythology has also been incorporated into the video game industry. Many video games have been developed that are based on Indian myths and legends. These games have been popular in India and around the world, and have helped to introduce a new generation of people to Indian mythology.

In addition, Indian mythology has also been incorporated into other forms of popular culture such as music, dance, and fashion. Many songs, dances and fashion styles have been inspired by Indian mythology and have become popular among people of all ages.

Indian mythology has played a significant role in popular culture, both in India and internationally. It has been adapted and incorporated into various forms of popular culture such as movies, television shows, comics, and video games. Indian mythology has also been incorporated into other forms of popular culture such as music, dance and fashion, and has been popular among people of all ages. This has helped to bring Indian mythology to a wider audience and has helped to introduce a new generation of people to these ancient stories and characters. The incorporation of Indian mythology into popular culture has also helped to preserve and promote India's rich cultural heritage and has helped to make it more accessible to people around the world. Indian mythology continues to be a major cultural influence in India and around the world, and its popularity in popular culture is a testament to its enduring relevance and appeal.

"Indian mythology provides a rich source of inspiration for contemporary artists and writers."

# XIV

# Comparisons and Connections with other mythological traditions

Indian mythology has many similarities and connections with other mythological traditions around the world. One of the most notable comparisons is with the mythologies of ancient Greece and Rome. Both Indian and Greek/Roman myths feature stories of gods and goddesses with superhuman powers, who intervene in the affairs of humans. They also share common themes such as love, war, and the struggle between good and evil.

Another comparison can be made with the mythology of ancient Egypt. Both Indian and Egyptian myths feature stories of creation, the afterlife and the worship of gods and goddesses with animal forms. They also share common themes such as the importance of the sun and the Nile river in their respective societies.

In addition, Indian mythology has connections with the mythology of other ancient cultures such as the Norse, Chinese and Mesoamerican. These myths share similar themes such as creation stories, the importance of ancestor worship, and the presence of a god or gods who are responsible for the cosmos.

Furthermore, Indian mythology also shares similarities with the mythology of other ancient cultures from Africa, Polynesia, and Australia. These myths share common themes such as creation stories, ancestor worship, and the presence of a god or gods who are responsible for the cosmos.

Indian mythology has many similarities and connections with other mythological traditions around the world. It shares many common themes with the mythologies of ancient Greece and Rome, ancient Egypt, Norse, Chinese and Mesoamerican cultures, and other ancient cultures from Africa, Polynesia, and Australia. These similarities and connections suggest that many of the universal human experiences, such as creation, the afterlife, and the relationship between humans and the divine, are reflected in the myths of different cultures. The study of Indian mythology in relation to other mythological traditions can provide a deeper understanding of the human experience and the role that myths play in shaping cultural beliefs and practices.

"The characters and events in Indian
mythology are not just stories, but also a
reflection of our human nature."

# XV

# Conclusion: The ongoing Relevance and Significance of Indian Mythology

Indian mythology is a rich and complex tradition that has played a significant role in shaping Indian culture and society for thousands of years. The stories and characters from Indian mythology continue to be widely read and studied, and have had a significant influence on art, literature, and popular culture.

The myths and legends of Indian mythology are not just ancient stories, but they contain deep wisdom and lessons that are still relevant today. They offer insights into the human experience and provide guidance for living a virtuous life. The psychological, feminist, ecological and postcolonial interpretations of these myths offer new perspectives and insights into these stories, making them even more relevant in the modern world.

The incorporation of Indian mythology into popular culture has helped to bring these ancient stories to a wider audience and has helped to preserve and promote India's rich cultural heritage. The popularity of Indian mythology in popular culture is a testament to its enduring relevance and appeal.

In addition, comparisons and connections with other mythological traditions around the world have highlighted the universal human experiences reflected in Indian myths and the role of myths in shaping cultural beliefs and practices.

Overall, Indian mythology continues to be a major cultural influence in India and around the world. Its ongoing relevance and significance are a testament to the timeless wisdom and lessons contained in these ancient stories.

# OTHER BOOKS OF THE AUTHOR

1. The Moments When I Met God
2. Kashiyile Theertha Pathangal
3. GURU GYAN VANI
4. Abhiprerak Gita
5. ASSI SE JAIN GHAT TAK
6. Hopelessness of Arjuna
7. The Soul and It's True Nature
8. Sense of Action (Karma)
9. Action through Wisdom
10. Action through Wisdom
11. THEORY AND PRACTICAL OF EVERY ACTION
12. LOGICAL UNDERSTANDING OF THE SUPREME
13. THE IMPERISHABLE SUPREME
14. Yatra Nishadraj se Hanuman Ghat Tak
15. Yatra Karnatak Ghat se Raja Ghat Tak
16. Yatra Pandey Ghat se Prayagraj Ghat Tak
17. Yatra Ranjendra Prasad Ghat se Dattatreya Ghat Tak
18. YaatraSindhiya Ghat se Gwaliar Ghat Tak
19. Yatra Mangala Gauri Ghat se Hanuman Gadhi Ghat Tak
20. Yatra Gaay Ghat Se Nishad Ghat Tak
21. MAA GANGA, GHATEN EVM UTSAV
22. Ganga Arti Dev Deepavali evam Any Utsav
23. Potentials of Digitalized India
24. VEDIC CONSCIOUSNESS
25. A Brief Introduction to Vedic Science
26. Kashi ke Barah Jyotirling
27. IMPACT OF MOTIVATION
28. Let's have a Milky Way Journey
29. Color Therapy in a Nutshell

30. Rigveda in a Nutshell
31. Yajurveda in a Nutshell
32. Samveda in a Nutshell
33. Atharva Veda in a Nutshell
34. Ayushman Bhava - Ayurveda
35. Srimad Bhagavad Gita and Upanishad Connection
36. Srimad Bhagavad Gita - an attempt to summarize each chapter.
37. Facts and Impact of Nakshatra
38. Astro Gems - NAVARATNA
39. Ekadashi - A Concise Overview
40. A Concise View of Hanuman Chalisa
41. Inspirational Gita
42. Nakshatraranyam
43. Summary of 18 Mahapuranas
44. Synopsis of 18 Upa Puranas
45. Rigvediya Upanishads
46. Shukla Yajurvediya Upanishads
47. Krishna Yajurvediya Upanishads
48. Samavediya Upanishads
49. Atharvavediya Upanishads
50. The Seven Great Sages
51. From Rocket Scientist to President Dr. APJ Abdul Kalam
52. The Visionary's Voice - Quotes of Dr. APJ Abdul Kalam
53. The Wisdom of Swami Vivekananda: Insights and Inspiration from a Legendary Spiritual Teacher
54. Ayurvedic Remedies from the Garden
55. Sages and Seers
56. Rising Strong – Motivational Stories of Women
57. Beyond Flames -Mystery stories of Funeral Ghat Manikarnika
58. The Origins of Tulsi: A Look at the Mythological Roots of the Plant"

90. Astrological Remedies
91. The Secret Power of Motivation
92. Secret of Developing your Inner Strength
93. The Secret Path to Motivation
94. The Art and Secret of Positive Thinking
95. The Secrets of Practicing Ethical Living
96. Indian Art and Painting
97. The Indian Herbalism
98. Bharatanatyam to Kathak
99. Exploring India's Astrological Remedies
100. The Indian Festival of Flowers
101. Indian Handicrafts
102. The Splashes of Joy – India's Colour Festival

# CONTACT

DR. JAGADEESH PILLAI

PhD in Vedic Science

Four Times Guinness World Record Holder

Winner of Mahatma Gandhi Vishwa Shanti Puraskar and
Global Peace Ambassador

Gemology, Astro & Vastu Consultant - Spiritual Counselor

Consultant for designing World Record Ideas

Efficient Tarot Card Reader

9839093003

myrichindia@gmail.com

drjagadeeshpillai@facebook

drjagadeeshpillai@instagram

jagadeeshpillai@youtube

www. JAGADEESHPILLAI.com

|| LOKAHA SAMASTHAHA SUKHINO BHAVANTU ||

* 9 7 9 8 8 8 8 9 5 1 8 0 1 3 *